Seymour Simon

BIG BUGS

SeaStar Books • San Francisco

To Benjamin and Joel

Front cover photograph: praying mantis

Title page photograph: lantern fly

Page 3 photograph: dragonfly

Permission to use the following photographs is gratefully acknowledged:

Front cover: © Tim Davis/Photo Researchers, Inc.; title page, pages 14–15: © Gary Retherford/Photo Researchers, Inc.; pages 2–3, 18–19: © Stephen Dalton/Photo Researchers, Inc.; pages 4–5, 16–17: © John Mitchell/Photo Researchers, Inc.; pages 6–7: © Bob Jensen/Bruce Coleman Inc.; pages 8–9, 20–21: © Gail Shumway/Bruce Coleman Inc.; pages 10–11: © Jane Burton/Bruce Coleman Inc.; pages 12–13: © Robert Shantz; pages 22–23: © Jeff Lepore/Photo Researchers, Inc.; pages 24–25:©Michael Lustbader/Photo Researchers, Inc.; pages 26–27: © Michael Fogden/AnimalsAnimals; pages 28–29: © John Mitchell/OSF/AnimalsAnimals; pages 30–31: © Tom McHugh/Photo Researchers, Inc.; page 32: © Michael Fogden/Bruce Coleman Inc; back cover: © David M. Dennis/AnimalsAnimals

Book design by E. Friedman.
Typeset in 22/40 ITC Century Book.
Manufactured in China.

SeaStar is an imprint of Chronicle Books LLC.

Library of Congress Cataloging-in-Publication Data
Simon, Seymour.
Big bugs / Seymour Simon.
p. cm. — (SeeMore readers)
1-58717-253-4 (Library Binding)
1-58717-265-8 (Paperback)
1. Insects—Size—Juvenile literature. 2. Arachnida—Size—Juvenile
literature. I. Title.
QL467.2.S567 2005
595.7—dc22
2004015285

Distributed in Canada by Raincoast Books
9050 Shaughnessy Street, Vancouver, British Columbia V6P 6E5

10 9 8 7 6 5 4 3 2 1

Chronicle Books LLC
85 Second Street, San Francisco, California 94105

www.chroniclekids.com

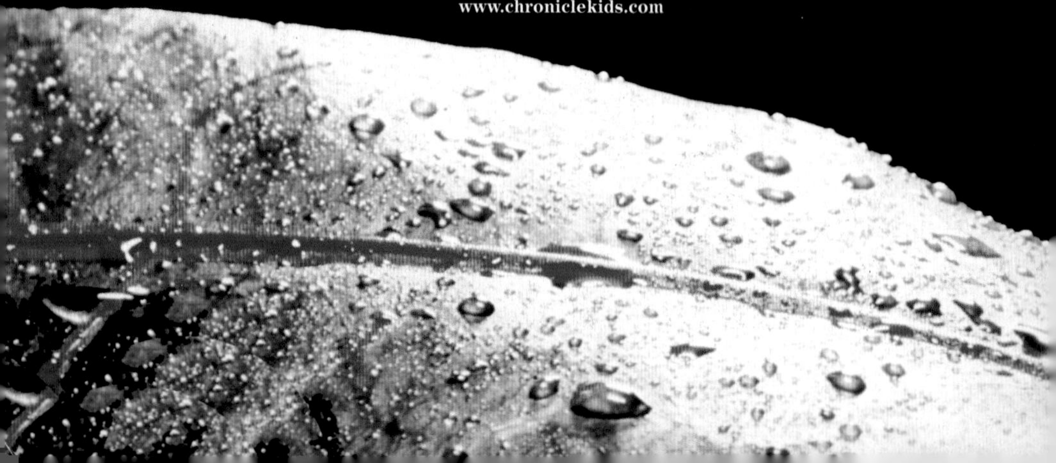

Bugs are a kind of insect.
Bugs have six legs, like other
insects such as beetles and
butterflies.
In this book we're going to
talk about big insects,
scorpions, and spiders that
people often think of as bugs.

The giant water bug is the largest bug in the world. A giant water bug can kill a frog or a fish twice its size.

The goliath beetle of West Africa is the heaviest insect in the world. It is over 4 inches long and weighs nearly $\frac{1}{4}$ pound.

That's about the size of an apple.

Despite their weight, goliath beetles are able to fly.

They zip through the air like bullets and can break glass windows.

Actual size

The giant cockroach of South America is the largest roach in the world.

Actual size

It is about 3 inches long.

It gives off an awful smell so

it won't be eaten by its enemies.

But some people keep giant

cockroaches as pets.

The bulldog ant of Australia is about 1½ inches long, about the size of your pinky. This ant has powerful jaws and a mean sting. Bulldog ants will attack anything that comes near their nest.

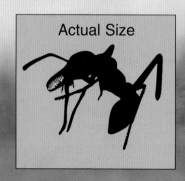

Actual Size

The female tarantula-hawk wasp stings a tarantula and paralyzes it. She lays her eggs on the tarantula.

Actual size

The eggs hatch in several days, and the young wasps feed on the body of the tarantula.

The lantern fly of South America
is about 3 inches long.
The top of its head looks
like an alligator.
The top of its head is
also hollow, like a peanut shell.
No one knows why.

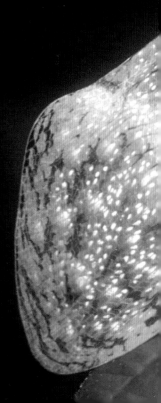

Actual size

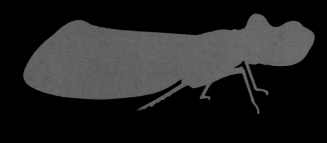

Robber flies can grow
to be 2 inches long,
with a 4-inch wingspan.
They hunt any flying
insect, even bees
and wasps.
The largest robber flies live
in South America or
Australia, but many large
robber flies live in the
United States.

Actual size

Huge dragonflies lived over 300
million years ago, long before
the dinosaurs.
They had wingspans of
30 inches, about the length
of a person's arm.
Most dragonflies today
have wingspans of 3 or 4 inches.
Dragonflies are great fliers
and can catch and eat insects
in midair.

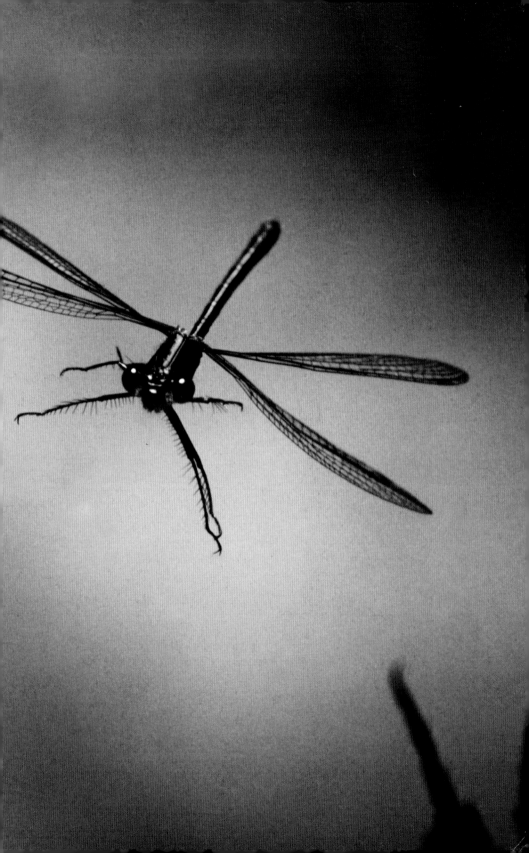

Birdwing butterflies are the biggest butterflies in the world. These colorful giants from Australia have a 12-inch wingspan.

They fly so fast that people can't catch them with nets. Instead, collectors try to knock them down with a blast of water.

Atlas is the name of a giant in early Greek legends. The atlas moth of Southeast Asia has a larger wing area than any other moth. Its wings cover about the same space as two pages of this book.

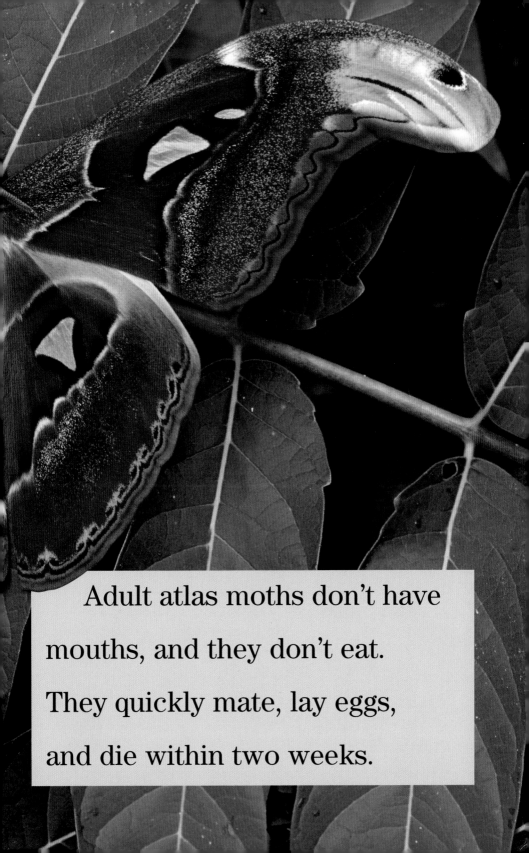

Adult atlas moths don't have mouths, and they don't eat. They quickly mate, lay eggs, and die within two weeks.

A praying mantis doesn't pray.

It is really waiting quietly for an

insect to pass by.

When a mantis catches an insect,

it feeds on it like a person eating

an ear of corn.

This walking stick is over 1 foot long and looks like a piece of dead wood.

It moves slowly at night and feeds on leaves.

Lizards, birds, and spiders will eat walking sticks, but they have a hard time spotting them.

The bird-eating spider of South America is the biggest spider in the world.

It is as large as your open hand.
Bird-eating spiders catch and eat
birds and other small animals.

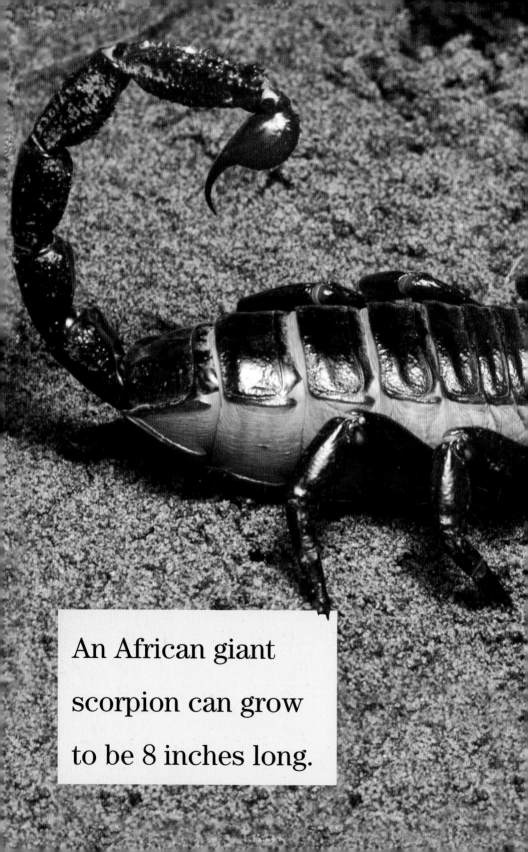

An African giant scorpion can grow to be 8 inches long.

The giant scorpion hunts for insects at night and tears them to pieces with its large claws.

Most bugs are tiny and weigh about as much as a feather.
The bugs in this book weigh dozens of times more than most other bugs.
That is why we call them big bugs.